TEN SiLLY SANTAS

spck

TEN SILLY SANTAS

AND OTHER CHRISTMAS POEMS

STEVE TURNER

ILLUSTRATED
BY
KATIE ABEY

First published in Great Britain in 2020

Society for Promoting Christian Knowledge
36 Causton Street, London SW1P 4ST
www.spck.org.uk

Text copywright © Steve Turner 2020
Illustrations © Katie Abey 2020

British Library Cataloguing-in-Publication Data
A catalogue record for this book is available from the British Library

ISBN 978-0-281-08375-6

Printed by Jellyfish Print Solutions
Subsequently digitally printed in Great Britain

Produced on paper from sustainable forests

CONTENTS

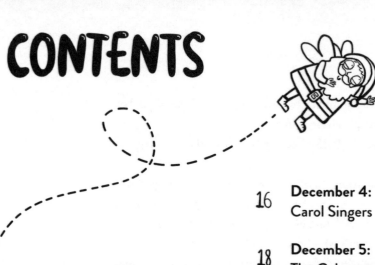

DECEMBER 1
COUNTING THE DAYS

I'm counting the days to Christmas
Twelve eleven ten
I'm counting the days to Christmas
When? When? When?

I'm counting the days to Christmas
Ten nine eight
I'm counting the days to Christmas
I can't wait!

I'm counting the days to Christmas
Eight seven six
I'm counting the days to Christmas
Five more ticks!

I'm counting the days to Christmas
Six five four
I'm counting the days to Christmas
Just three more.

I'm counting the days to Christmas
Four three two
I'm counting the days to Christmas
Why don't you?

I'm counting the days to Christmas
One one one
I'm counting the hours to Christmas
It's almost come.

I'm counting the days to Christmas
It's right here!
I'm counting the days to Christmas
(The one next year).

DECEMBER 2
ADVENT CALENDAR

Gabriel is calling
(open the door)
Mary is praying
(open the door)
Joseph is dreaming
(open the door)
The donkey is braying
(open the door).

The shepherds are watching
(open the door)
The sheepdogs are bounding
(open the door)
The angels are singing
(open the door)
The trumpets are sounding
(open the door).

The Romans are counting
(open the door)
The people are flocking
(open the door)
Bethlehem's swarming
(open the door)
The hotels are locking
(open the door).

The camels are rolling
(open the door)
The wise men are riding
(open the door)
King Herod is plotting
(open the door)
The bright star is guiding
(open the door).

All heaven is praising
(open the door)
A new dawn is breaking
(open the door)
The glory is shining
(open the door)
The devil is quaking
(open the door).

The sheep they are bleating
(open the door)
The stable is humming
(open the door)
The white doves are cooing
(open the door)
The saviour is coming
(open the door).

13

DECEMBER 3
THE PARTY

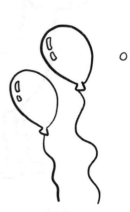
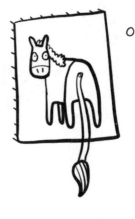

Passed the parcel
Lost my chair
Got blindfolded
Didn't care

Found the treasure
Pinned the tail
Bobbed the apple
Went to jail.

Ate the biscuits
Ate the buns
Ate the chocolates
Chewed the gums

Cracked the icing
Drank the Coke
Pulled the crackers
Got the joke.

Played the music
Scared the cats
Painted faces
Wore the hats

Hid in corners
Lost my phone
Grabbed my goodies
Walked back home.

15

DECEMBER 4
CAROL SINGERS

In days of yore
(that's not now, but before)
crowds of singers
would stand at the door
with candles in lanterns
and collect for the poor
while singing old songs
about what shepherds saw
when they heard bands of
angels and fell down in awe.

In days of yore
(that's not now, but before)
snowflakes would twist
through air that was raw
and top hats and bonnets
were what people wore
while singing old hymns
about what wise men saw
when they followed the star
to Bethlehem's door.

In days of yore
(that's not now, but before)
crowds of singers
would stand at the door
with sheets of music
and hand bells galore
while singing old songs
about what Mary saw
when she looked in the manger
at the child that she bore.

17

DECEMBER 5
THE COLOURS OF CHRISTMAS

Christmas is green
From what I could find
Christmas is green
As green as a pine.

No, Christmas is brown
Where Jesus was birthed
Christmas is brown
As brown as the earth.

Christmas is white
As Bing Crosby knows
Christmas is white
As white as the snows.

No, Christmas is black
In fields without light
Christmas is black
As black as the night.

Christmas is red
For Christmas is merry
Christmas is red
As red as a berry.

No, Christmas is blue
When Mary's in town
Christmas is blue
As blue as a gown.

19

DECEMBER 6
THE BELLS

Some bells wobble
Some bells roll
Some bells thunder
Some bells toll

Some bells ripple
Some bells plink
Some bells chinkle
Some bells clink.

Some bells tinkle
Some bells ching
Some bells jingle
Some bells ring

Some bells rattle
Some bells bang
Some bells jangle
Some bells clang.

Some bells clatter
Some bells clong
Some bells ding-ding
Some bells dong

Some bells shudder
Some bells ping
Some bells chatter
Some bells sing.

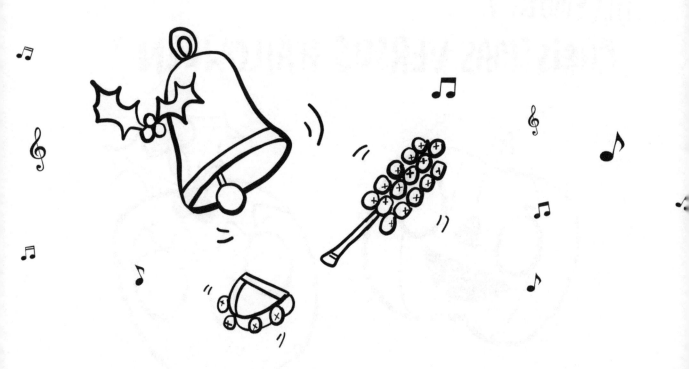

DECEMBER 7
CHRISTMAS VERSUS HALLOWEEN

There are no bones
At Christmas
Except in turkeys and chickens.
There are no ghosts
At Christmas
Except in stories by Dickens.

There is no blood
At Christmas
Except what is flowing within.
There are no skulls
At Christmas
Except what is under your skin.

There are no shocks
At Christmas
Except when unwrapping a toy.
There are no screams
At Christmas
Except of excitement and joy.

There are no knives
At Christmas
Except those for carving up meat.
There are no tricks
At Christmas
For everything's totally treat.

23

DECEMBER 8
DEEP INTO WINTER

Deep into winter
We all have to go
Deep into darkness
Deep into snow.

Deep into darkness
Deep into snow
Old things are dying
New things will grow.

Old things are dying
New things will grow
Deep into winter
We all have to go.

25

DECEMBER 9
PANTO

Panto was my intro to theatre
To footlights, drama, applause.
Some men would dress up as ladies
Some girls would come on as boys.

I recall their colourful clothing
Hair that was blue to its roots
I recall the thick paint on faces
The red lips, noses and boots.

There were princesses, widows and thieves
Pussycats, dimwits and dames
There were genies that leapt out of lamps
If someone mentioned their names.

There was singing, booing and laughter
Riddles and puzzles and jokes
There were frogs that turned into princes
Pumpkins that went up in smoke.

The baddies had skin that was greenish
Tongues that were pointed and long
The goodies were glowing like lightbulbs
They never could put a foot wrong.

The audience screamed with approval
Or let out a snake-like hiss
They'd all shout 'Look out it's behind you!'
'Oh no it's not!' 'Yes, it is.'

Panto was my intro to theatre
To curtains, costumes and stage
To abracadabra and magic
To words brought alive from a page.

DECEMBER 10
THE SCHOOL NATIVITY

ZZZZ

The shepherds see a blinding light
The cattle come in herds
The little lambs have lost their ears
The angel's lost for words.

The stable starts to shake a bit
A wise man drops his gift
The innkeeper is off with flu
The star begins to drift.

Then Joseph waves to Mum and Dad
Who think their boy's fantastic
Jesus plays it meek and mild, but
Then he would; he's plastic.

29

DECEMBER 11
MiAOWY CHRISTMAS

My cat likes giving at Christmas
so, I've made him a coat of red
I've built a sleigh out of matchsticks
and put a hat upon his head.

With white fluff on his furry face
and boots of black on his paws
I call him Father Whiskermas
or, as he prefers, Santa Claws.

31

DECEMBER 12
HOLLY

Sharp thorns:
The crown of Christ.

Red berries:
The blood of Christ.

Flamed shape:
The love of Christ.

Green leaves:
The life of Christ.

DECEMBER 13
iCiCLE

I saw an icicle
Ride upon a bicycle.
An icicle?
A bicycle?
That doesn't seem picycle.
In fact,
It's physically impicycle
For an icicle to bike.

If an icicle should decidycle
To ride
Upon a bicycle
The icicle would diecycle
And the bicycle would bang.

But I saw an icicle
Ride upon a bicycle
With a Sugar Puff, a Ricicle
And a box of Shredded Wheat.

DECEMBER 14
CRACKERS

Crackers are never loud enough for me.
They make a snapping sound,
like a twig being broken,
rather than the boom or bang
of gunpowder on fire.

Crackers are never cool enough for me.
They're too straight and round.
They look like sausages
wrapped in crepe and foil.

Crackers are never generous
enough for me.
I don't need:

a small key ring
a small paperclip
a small notepad
and a small moustache.

Paper hats make me look dull.

Crackers are never funny enough for me.
I don't want to guess what snowmen eat.
I don't care why the reindeer felt sad.
I don't have the time to say
'Brilliant bouncy Brussels sprouts'
ten times quickly.

Question: When is a joke not a joke?

Answer: When it comes from a cracker.

DECEMBER 15
OUR FIRST CHRISTMAS WITHOUT YOU

Your favourite chair will be empty
The voice that we loved we won't hear
There won't be your kisses and wishes
On labels we read out this year.

We won't get to buy you a present
We won't need to fear you got missed
But we'd rather be shopping for you
Than crossing your name off our list.

The day you once lit will be darker
The room will be quieter too
Our Christmas wish, if there is one,
Would be one more Christmas with you.

DECEMBER 16
MARY'S SONG

You tell me that his father's God
That I'm the chosen maid
You see the look upon my face
But say, 'Don't be afraid.'

So, Gabriel's your name, you say,
And heaven's where you're from
You've come to give me news, you say,
About my soon-born son.

So, Mary is my name, I say,
And Nazareth's my town
I'll give you what I've got to give
And lay my worries down.

You tell me that this baby child
That swims around within
Will one day be a holy thief
Who'll rob the world of sin.

So, Jesus is his name, you say,
He'll grow up to be strong.
I'll keep this news inside my heart
Then breathe it out in song.

DECEMBER 17

TOP OF THE TREE

I'm a fairy
on the top of a tree.
Please get me down
I'm in need of a wee.

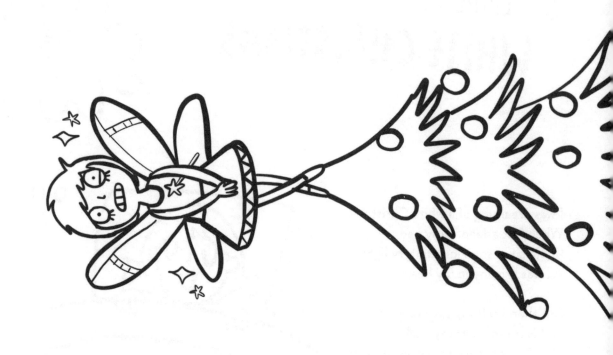

DECEMBER 18
WHITE CHRISTMAS

I was dreaming of a white Christmas
While fast asleep in my bed
Snowflakes spun in a wintery light
All was pristine in my head.

But then I felt my tingling toes
A shiver ran down my back
My pillows turned into piles of slush
The sheet was so cold it cracked.

The mattress became a block of ice
The duvet, it was freezing
I skidded across from side to side
Blowing my nose and sneezing.

I needed to have another dream
That would help me sort things out
I dreamt I was in the Sahara
During a summer of drought.

The snow started to melt away
The bedding began to dry
I felt the sand between my toes
And saw the blue of the sky.

So I'll dream of a gold Christmas
Where things are sunny and bright
It may not be as picturesque
But it'll keep me warm at night.

45

DECEMBER 19
TEN SILLY SANTAS

Ten silly Santas
At the north North Pole
One Santa cracked the ice
And fell down through a hole.

Nine silly Santas
Working in a shed
One Santa hit his thumb
And had to go to bed.

Eight silly Santas
All fired up to go
One Santa crashed his sleigh
And lost it in the snow.

Seven silly Santas
Learning how to fly
One Santa snapped his strap
And tumbled through the sky.

Six silly Santas
Sailing miles and miles
One Santa clipped a roof
And crashed on to the tiles.

Five silly Santas
In a chimney stack
One Santa tore his pants
So had to go straight back.

Four silly Santas
Creeping in the dark
One Santa woke the dog
And couldn't stop its bark.

Three silly Santas
Filling up a sock
One Santa found a foot
And fainted from the shock.

Two silly Santas
Riding round and round
One Santa fell asleep
And landed upside down.

One silly Santa
Gliding through the mist
Wrote a letter to himself
Then gave himself a gift.

DECEMBER 20
CHRISTMAS IS EVERYWHERE

It's Christmas in the USA
It's Christmas in Peru
It's Christmas in Nigeria
And in the Arctic too.

It's Christmas on the mountaintops
It's Christmas out at sea
It's Christmas in the forest dark
Where tigers take their tea.

It's Christmas over Disneyland
It's Christmas in Cologne
It's Christmas up the Eiffel Tower
(Unless the lights have blown).

It's Christmas in the chiming church
It's Christmas at the mall
It's Christmas on the skating rink
And in the village hall.

It's Christmas on the windowpanes
It's Christmas on the walls
It's Christmas in the tiny cracks
Where only glitter falls.

It's Christmas in the atmosphere
It's Christmas in the air
It's Christmas deep inside of me
It's Christmas everywhere.

49

DECEMBER 21
WHAT NOT TO BUY ME

Don't buy me knickers
Don't buy me socks
Don't give me small things
Inside a big box.

Don't buy me brushes
Don't buy a comb
Don't buy me schoolbooks
To work on at home.

Don't buy me ribbons
Don't buy me bows
Don't buy me tissues
To dab at my nose.

Don't buy me stickers
Don't buy me stamps
Don't buy me paper
For letters of thanks.

Don't buy me dusters
Don't buy me spray
Don't buy me cleaners
That take stains away.

Don't buy me cufflinks
Don't buy me ties
Don't buy me earmuffs.
Buy me: a surprise.

DECEMBER 22
THE BEST THINGS IN LIFE

I will give you a lamp of moonlight
and a necklace of stars.

I will give you the art of a sunrise
and a butterfly's wing.

I will give you a firework of thunder
and a sparkler of sun.

I will give you the perfume of flowers
and the spray of morning mist.

I will give you a cloak of fallen leaves
and a helmet of snow.

I will wrap my gifts in sheets of lightning,
label them with clouds,
and tie them with bows of rain.

53

DECEMBER 23
CHRISTMAS WRAPPING

Coloured paper
Ribbons
Bling
Gluey fixer
Scissors
String.

Piles of presents
Stickers
Bags
Season's Greetings
Glitter
Tags.

54

Tearing, cutting,
Folding
Stick
Wrapping, tying,
Labels
Lick.

Tubes and parcels
Boxes
Send
Messy table
Rubbish
End.

55

DECEMBER 24
THE RULES FOR SANTA

Here are the rules for Santa
With gifts for girls and boys
He mustn't ride his sleigh at night
In case he makes a noise.
Rooftops aren't for parking on
(Watch out for yellow lines)
Chimneys aren't for climbing down
Intruders will be fined.

Here are the rules for Santa
These are the hours to keep
He needs to take a break each shift
Or else he'll fall asleep.
Lifting up those heavy sacks
Might put his health at risk.
He could strain a shoulder blade
Or slip a spinal disc.

Here are the rules for Santa
Regarding codes of dress
His whiskers are superfluous
And make him look a mess.
Extra weight will have to go
It's bad to be too fat
And only imitation fur
Should line his coat and hat.

These are the rules for Santa
With which he must comply
Or else he'll lose his licence
And won't be free to fly.
His gifts will be impounded
We'll confiscate his sleigh
And Santa will be kept in jail
From now 'til Boxing Day.

DECEMBER 25

WHOSE BIRTHDAY IS CHRISTMAS?

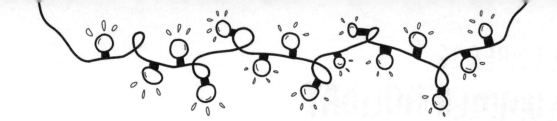

Whose birthday is Christmas
Whose songs do we sing
Whose lights are we lighting
Whose bells do we ring?

Whose birthday is Christmas
Whose crib's on display
Whose joy do we wish for
Whose peace do we say?

Whose birthday is Christmas
Whose party is thrown
Whose work do we honour
Whose love has been shown?

Whose birthday is Christmas
Whose feast do we eat
Whose gift do we open
Whose life do we greet?

DECEMBER 26
SUMMER HOLIDAY PLANS

Mum wants a holiday with water
and golden plots of sand.
Nan wants a holiday with card games
so she can show her hand.

Dad wants a holiday with mountains
that he can climb each day.
Pap wants a holiday with deckchairs
so he can drift away.

Lee wants a holiday with Lego
so he can build a house.
Di wants a holiday with Disney
so she can meet a mouse.

I want a holiday with wonder
that fills my head with awe.
I want a holiday with magic
that no one's seen before.

THE BEST PART OF CHRISTMAS

I saw it approaching
But it went by so fast
How long was it there for?
How long did it last?

Was it only around
So we could unwrap?
Was all the excitement
No more than a trap?

I looked forward so much
To Christmas this year
But as quick as it came
It then disappeared.

My presents seem lonely
Inside their big box
The once fattened stockings
Have flattened like socks.

The best part of Christmas
I now have to say
Is waiting for Christmas
Not Christmas Day.

DECEMBER 31
WHERE DID THE OLD YEAR GO?

Where did the old year go
Where did the old year go
We count it out
We count it out
Where did the old year go?

Why did the old year stop
Why did the old year stop
We count it out
We count it out
Why did the old year stop?

Who did the old year bless
Who did the old year bless
We count it out
We count it out
Who did the old year bless?

When will the new year start
When will the new year start
We count it in
We count it in
When will the new year start?

What will the new year bring
What will the new year bring
We count it in
We count it in
What will the new year bring?

How will the new year end
How will the new year end
We count it in
We count it in
How will the new year end?

The new year will end like this
The new year will end like this
We count it in
We count it out
The new year will end like this.

JANUARY 1
NEW YEAR'S RESOLUTIONS

I will look after my room
I will tidy and dust
I will put things in place
I must, I must.

I will do all my homework
I will draw up a plan
I will listen to teachers
I can, I can.

I will cut down on junk food
I will cut down on fat
I will exercise daily
I'll do that, I'll do that.

I will recycle rubbish
I will save the world now
I will help poorer children
I vow, I vow.

I will be nice to people
I will learn a new skill
I will keep resolutions
I will, I will.

JANUARY 2
BROKEN RESOLUTIONS

I have filthied my bedroom
I have broken a chair
I have left things on floors
I don't care, I don't care.

I have scoffed double burgers
I have pigged out on grease
I have slouched on the sofa
I'm obese, I'm obese.

I have cheated with homework
I have skipped days off school
I have blanked out my teachers
I'm so cool, I'm so cool.

I have littered the pavements
I have let the world rot
I have walked by the starving
I can't stop, I can't stop.

I have been rude to people
I have learned nothing new
I break resolutions
Yes I do, yes I do.

JANUARY 5
CHRISTMAS IS OVER

Christmas is all over
The day the cards get ripped
Baubles go in boxes
The dying tree gets stripped.

Candles lie in bundles
A missing star is found
Glitter falls in dust piles
The lights are wrapped and wound.

Peace goes in the attic
Goodwill goes out the door
Great joy gets put in storage
Glad tidings in a drawer.

Wise men pack their presents
The angels hold their tongues
But where do we put Jesus
Until next Christmas comes?

71

STEVE TURNER

Steve Turner is a performance poet, journalist, biographer and author of critically acclaimed anthologies of children's verse. Among his bestselling books for children are *The Day I Fell Down the Toilet and Other Poems* (Lion, 1997) and *Don't Take Your Elephant to School* (Lion, 2006). He has appeared in over a hundred poetry anthologies, including *The Oxford Book of Christmas Poems* (OUP, 1999), *100 Best Poems for Children* (Puffin, 2002), *The Oxford Book of Children's Poetry* (OUP, 2007), *Essential Poems for Children* (HarperCollins, 2005) and *Happy Poems* (Macmillan Children's Books, 2018), and has work included on the GCSE syllabuses of two examination boards.

Steve started writing poetry in 1965, and published a collection ten years later that was greeted by the *Daily Mail* with the headline 'At last, a poet who captures today with all the flair of a rock number.' He has since read his work in schools, colleges, libraries, music venues and at festivals in the UK, Europe and America. *The Day I Fell Down the Toilet* became one of the bestselling books of contemporary poetry for children, with sales in excess of 130,000. Dinah Hall of the *Sunday Telegraph* called him 'One of the most original and child-friendly voices to emerge in the last few years.'

KATIE ABEY

Katie Abey is an illustrator human who lives in a teeny hobbit-like house in Derbyshire with a cat, a hedgehog and a husband. Her work provides illustrative doses of happiness and motivation along with a little dash of sarcasm. She is a big lover of animals and her work often features creatures looking slightly nonchalant, perturbed or even a bit deranged.

She likes using a lot of colour in her work and this love of colour is reflected in her brightly coloured studio space and her hair, which frequently changes colour to match its surroundings. When Katie is not drawing awkward cats and llamas she enjoys yoga, reading and referring to herself in the third person.

DRAW YOUR OWN!

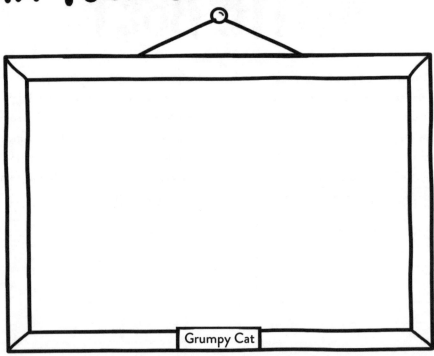

Grumpy Cat

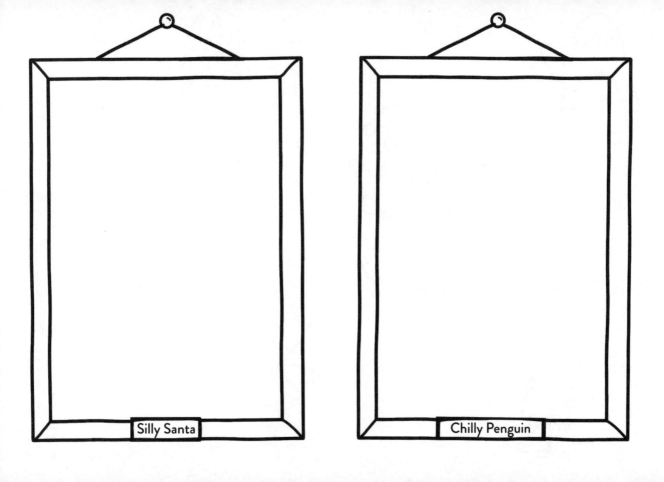

Silly Santa

Chilly Penguin